W0010548

pocket posh®

· · · · · · · · · ·

take care

Inspired Activities
for **Reflection**

pocket posh

· · · · · · · · · ·

take care

Inspired Activities
for **Reflection**

Andrews McMeel
PUBLISHING®

We all need some time to focus on ourselves. It's easy to become overwhelmed—by work, by home responsibilities, by the news of the day. It's important to step away, relax, and recenter. *Take Care: Inspired Activities for Reflection* invites you to practice small moments of self-care through mindful activities, inspirational words, and thought-provoking journal prompts. Take some time for yourself.

. . . take care.

"Don't be pushed
by your problems.
Be led by your
dreams."

—*Ralph Waldo Emerson*

```
C S M N T C V V S V S C O U C H E S C B
O I S R O M A M A C C H I A T O I S Z E
F C B C R L U F S A N D W I C H E S T G
F E X F R V C S F B Y L L L C I U A U Y
E D H L N O K M I E G B S F H T L T M O
E C O A C V I E U C A B A T H O T Y O W
B O M V Y A U S J F S M O R C A L A C I
E F E O S B F A S E F O E O I X H C H F
A F M R Y U D F N A M I H R X S A V A I
N E A E H R D O E S N C N O I E T F A A
S E D D A X C T T L T T N S T C O A C C
O S E S J S T I B O A I S I K B A Q A C
D P S Y I O U U H A C T A A V H W N M E
A A O R H R F A P C F H T V U T H E O S
K S U U F S O I U W C I U E E M O O V S
H T P P A P H P T O D T W P O C Q T I O
G R Z S E X P C Z E Z S O X A Q F A K S
G I R M K A G R I L L E D P A N I N I G
T E D H C B I S C O T T I I S Y Y F S Y
I S Z O E S P R E S S O G E E T F C M H
```

coffeehouse

BARISTA	ESPRESSO	MOCHA
BISCOTTI	FLAVORED SYRUPS	MUFFINS
CAFFE AMERICANO	FRUIT SMOOTHIES	MUSIC
CAFFE LATTE	GRILLED PANINI	PASTRIES
CAPPUCCINO	HOMEMADE SOUP	SANDWICHES
CHAI TEA	HOT CHOCOLATE	SCONES
COFFEE BEANS	HOT TEA	WI-FI ACCESS
COUCHES	ICED COFFEE	
CROISSANTS	MACCHIATO	

positive spin

Focusing on the positive is an easy way to give your mental and emotional reserves a boost. Take a page from *The Sound of Music* and work on your own version of the song "My Favorite Things." Write down five things—no matter how small—that make you happy.

. . . .

. . . .

. . . .

. . . .

. . . .

. . . .

. . . .

. . . .

. . . .

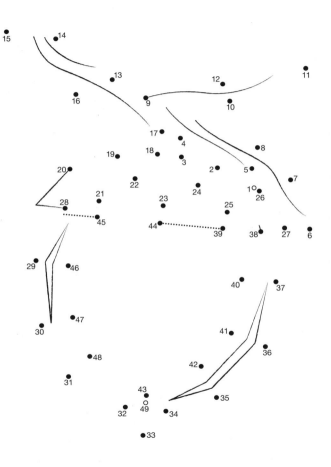

looking back to look forward

How have you grown in the last five years? What positive changes have you made in your life? Think about how you can apply your experience to grow further five years from now.

"When you recover or discover something that nourishes your soul and brings joy, care enough about yourself to make room for it in your life."

—*Jean Shinoda Bolen*

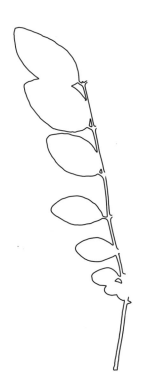

ARTS By Anna Gundlach

ACROSS

1. Flatten out
5. Not-so-common payment method, these days
11. Parks of civil rights fame
12. South Pacific island
13. Southern term of respect
14. NYC museum where you can see Monet's "Water Lily Pond"
15. Off-kilter
17. Fair-hiring inits.
18. London museum where you can see Warhol's "Marylin Diptych"
22. Like a stadium at an exciting game
23. NYC museum where you can see Pollock's "alchemy"
28. Grp. that creates a code of ethics for lawyers
29. "Confessions" singer
31. Paris museum where you can see Da Vinci's "Mona Lisa"
35. More than none, but fewer than most
36. Creature's home, in old horror movies
37. Atop
38. Simmered slowly
39. Chilean coin

DOWN

1. "The Joy of Cooking" writer Rombauer
2. Cook on a spit
3. Panasonic's HQ's location
4. Sticker worn at a convention
5. Uncle Fester's cousin
6. "Don't think so"
7. Revolutionary figure on many a t-shirt
8. Singer-songwriter Mann
9. Do the driving
10. Flirt with
16. Used to be
19. Planner abbr.
20. Honolulu's home
21. Get togged
23. Really ticks off
24. WWII threat
25. Speedometer, e.g.
26. "If all goes according to plan ..."
27. Inter-office notes
30. "The Biggest Little City In The World"
32. Solemn pledge
33. Wade's legal opponent
34. This clue's position, in this puzzle

"And the day came when the risk to remain tight in a bud was more painful than the risk it took to blossom."

—*Anaïs Nin*

```
Z  G  N  Z  J  Y  A  R  E  F  L  E  C  T  I  O  N  J  Z  N
P  M  N  E  Q  S  G  W  A  T  E  R  F  A  L  L  S  S  M  O
Q  Y  R  X  F  F  A  M  X  X  C  C  E  D  D  N  X  J  X  P
V  T  U  N  E  J  Y  S  S  R  U  G  E  P  L  C  B  U  U  T
R  H  Q  B  U  M  P  J  A  I  N  R  A  X  P  C  C  Z  S  I
W  O  K  V  H  H  R  J  H  A  O  S  A  Y  S  L  X  X  U  C
A  L  T  S  P  Q  I  I  R  L  E  P  R  E  C  H  A  U  N  A
T  O  X  H  K  V  D  O  O  V  M  T  V  I  S  A  D  R  L  L
E  G  B  E  X  Y  E  C  S  S  P  W  Y  N  Q  J  Y  I  I  I
R  Y  L  L  D  Y  I  D  L  E  F  V  I  I  D  Q  N  Q  G  L
D  P  U  L  I  T  B  Z  O  C  C  A  J  U  R  O  O  C  H  L
R  S  E  M  L  D  L  G  H  P  T  R  P  H  N  F  D  H  T  U
O  P  B  U  M  Q  I  Q  I  N  T  Z  E  E  Q  Q  J  P  T  S
P  E  M  X  V  D  A  L  U  P  L  Y  M  T  I  V  I  R  K  I
L  C  U  L  N  Y  C  O  G  W  B  O  C  S  H  F  R  X  Q  O
E  T  C  I  G  E  F  N  V  V  N  R  K  I  U  I  R  Y  L  N
T  R  W  I  R  L  E  F  R  E  D  Z  R  E  N  D  D  D  G  B
N  U  Y  C  E  L  O  Q  H  U  O  P  C  U  X  K  M  I  F  J
K  M  V  W  E  O  J  P  P  O  T  O  F  G  O  L  D  T  N  H
A  L  E  W  N  W  V  I  O  L  E  T  L  I  G  H  T  F  U  G
```

rainbow

ARC	MULTICOLORED	SKY
BLUE	MYTHOLOGY	SPECTRUM
END	OPTICAL ILLUSION	SUNLIGHT
FOUNTAINS	ORANGE	VIOLET
GAY PRIDE	PHENOMENON	WATER DROPLET
GREEN	POT OF GOLD	WATERFALL
INDIGO	RED	YELLOW
LEPRECHAUN	REFLECTION	
LIGHT	SECRET HIDING	

find and circle

Five sports	⊙○○○○
Five words starting and ending in "H"	○○○○○
Three five-letter words rhyming with "mound"	○○○
J. Edgar ____	○
Pizza foundation	○

"If you try to follow
everyone else and be
like everyone else,
before you know it
you're gone. You're
not going to find
yourself again; you'll
just be a version of
what you might have
hoped to have been."

—*Dolly Parton*

gratitude for growth

We all experience failure at some point in our lives. But learning from our stumbles can lead to the greatest personal growth. Reflect on an experience that was negative at the time, but that you are grateful for in some way now.

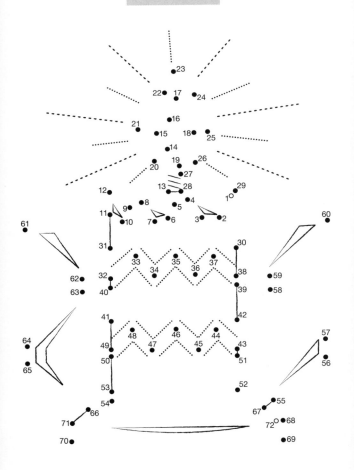

connecting threads

There are people in our lives who lift us up—whose support and love make us better. Who are those people for you? Write down their names and then reach out to them in some way. It's a great way to express gratitude and strengthen connections.

. . . .

. . . .

. . . .

. . . .

. . . .

. . . .

. . . .

. . . .

. . . .

"There are two ways of spreading light: to be the candle, or the mirror that reflects it."

—*Edith Wharton*

imagination By Anna Gundlach

ACROSS

1. Cartoonishly conks on the noggin
5. Drink up
11. And nothing more
12. Sips slowly
13. Huge fan of, slangily
14. Between-radio-stations noise
15. Using your imagination to form a new idea
17. Joe of "Home Alone"
18. Yuletide drink
19. Metal-bearing rock
21. Loafed
24. Texas battle site
28. Using your imagination to form a new idea
31. Mogadishu resident
32. Singer above tenor
33. "Tada!"
34. Germ of an idea
35. Like llamas
36. Banks of talk shows and fashion shows

DOWN

1. Pear option
2. Winning
3. Tarmax taxi
4. Aligns (with)
5. Being stimulated to be inventive and imaginative
6. Dog of no particular breed
7. Source of imagination
8. "Are not" retort
9. Are
10. PC panic button
16. "Green" prefix
20. Lilly of pharmaceuticals
21. Show contempt for
22. Set, like an alarm
23. Give a hard time to
25. Piratey "Hold it!"
26. "Wrecking Ball" singer Cyrus
27. Cute water mammal
29. Utah ski site
30. Baby ___ (popular Star Wars character)
31. Place for a soak and a massage

"You can only work on yourself. Start there."

—*Alice O. Howell*

```
W A F M Y D F H O C B E G D T I W N W V
F L A Z J U P L E G L P P A B T Z J Q B
A B C V E C F R Y G O I B I S B N B U F
T A Y E Z K A E A C M O P E B C O X I F
K T J G F R L E N I A R B P T O X Q C W
R R A N C K N U M T R T W A J E R V L A
T O P F C E W D I D V I C F R N H T J R
P S H A D H R Z T Q C H E H K N A D Q B
N S R L A A I A Y N A M O F E E O G B L
V G O R L O U C R A N E C S A R H W R E
X G K L Y J F V J M H D O I P L Y X L R
B M A B H U M M I N G B I R D R C U E J
J M F O R I O L E D I P P E R R E O J O
H D S N O W Y E G R E T U A C A B Y N M
C L W L W C A R D I N A L R V D O V E N
A D T O C B N K B L U E B I R D O O K U
D I A V K T C G O O S E L Y U R B C G R
C B L A C K B I R D E G F D E K Y R O P
R N F R P C H I C K A D E E T T Z O A T
B A V P L H O U S E F I N C H R M W J I
```

birds

ALBATROSS
BARN OWL
BLACKBIRD
BLUEBIRD
BOOBY
CARDINAL
CHICKADEE
CRANE
CROW

DIPPER
DOVE
DUCK
FLYCATCHER
GOLDEN EAGLE
GOOSE
GRACKLE
HOUSE FINCH
HUMMINGBIRD

IBIS
MALLARD
ORIOLE
OSPREY
PRAIRIE FALCON
SNOWY EGRET
WARBLER

expanding horizons

Sometimes getting away from our day-to-day lives offers a much-needed change in perspective. Have you ever traveled anywhere that changed you? Reflect on that place and your connection to it.

....

....

....

....

....

....

....

....

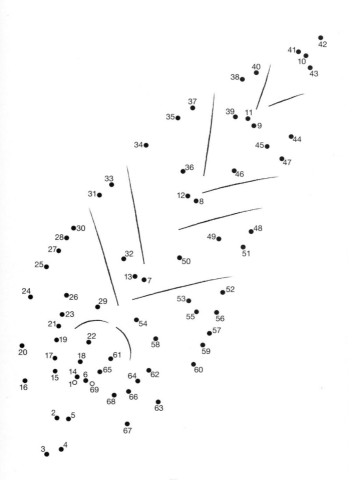

31

the power of "yes"

What would you say "yes" to if you had more time? Is there a project you've been putting off or a skill you've always wanted to learn? Reflect on one of these stretch goals. To accomplish it, what would the first step be? Can you take that first step?

. . . .

. . . .

. . . .

. . . .

. . . .

. . . .

. . . .

. . . .

. . . .

"Nothing in life
is to be feared;
it is only to be
understood.
Now is the time
to understand
more so that we
may fear less."

—*Marie Curie*

Nature By Anna Gundlach

ACROSS

1. Immediate danger
6. GI support grp.
9. Hawaii's biggest form of income
12. It's left in a barista's jar
13. Protrusion on a scarab beetle or VW Beetle
14. Inventor Whitney
15. Final (abbr.)
16. School support org.
17. Haunted house sounds
20. Does not posssess
22. With 23-Across, a relaxing place for rest represented by this puzzle's circled squares
23. See 22-Across
24. "The Age of Innocence" author Wharton
26. Potter's oven
27. Like the wood in a bonfire
28. Fish in a poke bowl
30. DC summer clock setting
31. Gives a new moniker to
36. Gathering for spelling or quilting
37. "Ideas worth spreading" lecture
38. Feeling blue
39. Like the air around a bonfire

DOWN

1. School support org.
2. A long, long time
3. Boring routine
4. Miffed state
5. Comic strip character with a security blanket
6. Spork, e.g.
7. Letter found at the end of autumn
8. Potent painkiller
10. Weekly comedy show since 1975, for short
11. PEMDAS subject
17. "I wouldn't do that if I were you..."
18. Left out
19. Pick
21. "___ was saying ..."
22. Paparazzi follow them
25. Melissa Joan of "Sabrina the Teenage Witch"
26. Sorts
29. Little titter bit
32. Check deposit spot, for short
33. Chinese leader with a "Little Red Book"
34. Bugling beast
35. Beautiful view on a sunny hike

"Obstacles don't
block the path.
They are the path."

—*Zen proverb*

```
U S T N A D M I S S I O N S P E B Q I I
A C Q U I S I T I O N S D Y J X X Q R C
T U Y Z F M K E H S A Q G O L C T Z B N
I L N A T U R A L L I G H T N L O B G S
O P P H O T O G R A P H Y S A O U J A Q
A T C V G S E C U R I T Y G U A R D L T
A U O O X R X D U L N Z Z U D A G S L L
R R L L I G H F A Z S V K V I Q U W E N
C E L U U F I C X E T A N B O Y I E R E
H H E N R M B B R S A H Z D G P D H Y Y
I C C T X K I E R M L K L H U C E D R Y
T U T E B T T E H L L Z B M I Q S A T J
E R I E R S T P T I A E C E D A R I R U
C A O R U S O E C Q T C J V E B N Z K Y
T T N A A H I Z A E I R O W I U B N H Z
U O B M S U D C H U O E N L M D S S H K
R R H T Q W A N O H N M L M P I E C E S
E O F T Z R E Y F K V M O D E R N O T Z
O I L P A I N T I N G C A O O Z J A U I
G C L A S S I C A L H F N L F S V X T T
```

art museum

ACQUISITIONS
ADMISSIONS
ARCHITECTURE
AUDIO GUIDE
AUSTERE
CLASSICAL
COLLECTION
COMMUNITY
CURATOR
DONORS

EXHIBIT
GALLERY
GIFT SHOP
INSTALLATION
LIBRARY
MASTERS
MODERN
NATURAL LIGHT
OIL PAINTING
ON LOAN

PHOTOGRAPHY
PIECES
QUIET
SCULPTURE
SECURITY GUARD
TOUR GUIDES
VIDEO
VOLUNTEER

find and circle

Five four-letter colors	⊘○○○○
Five countries starting with "P"	○○○○○
The Who founding members Pete and Roger	○○
Two words formed from A-C-E-N-O	○○
Two four-letter units of time	○○

"The world is changed by your example, not by your opinion."

—*Paulo Coelho*

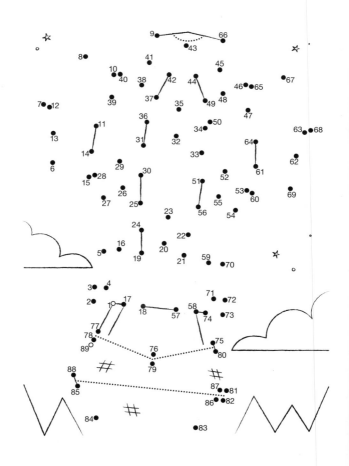

"We can choose to be affected
by the world or we can choose
to affect the world."

—*Heidi Wills*

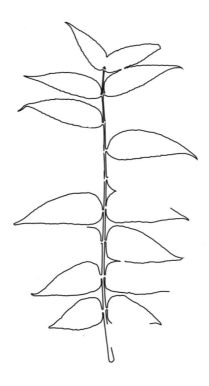

nourishment By Anna Gundlach

ACROSS

1. Gardener's pest
6. "You are not!" rejoinder
11. Get ready for impact
12. Topper on some wedding cakes
13. Nourishing meals not found in restaurants
15. ___-Wan Kenobi
16. Frequently, poetically
17. Bread like pita and naan
19. They're bumped in some hellos
23. The process of being nourished
25. Of the eye
26. Sounds like a baby
28. Capital of Peru?
30. Abbr. following comp and poli
31. Meals that provide a sense of nostalgic well-being
36. Grumpy or Sneezy
37. Older, witchy woman
38. Decorative bit in Times New Roman, but not Arial
39. Sharpens

DOWN

1. Completely detest
2. Free, like some legal services
3. Really overact
4. Rocks from a bartender
5. Early 20th century art movement, informally
6. Outfielder's yell
7. Keeper of pairs of bears, hares, and mares
8. "Me?," to Miss Piggy
9. Anderson Cooper, to Gloria Vanderbilt
10. "Holy cow!," on Twitter
14. Armed forces member with authority
18. Addams Family cousin
20. [quoted as originally written]
21. "Can we joke about that yet?"
22. Carnival treat similar to shave ice
24. Terrible deal
27. School Crossing sign's quintet
29. Make indelible marks
31. Outdated audio media
32. Need to pay back
33. Scratch the surface of
34. End of many 9-5 work wks.
35. Counterpart of "to"

"What you do makes
a difference, and you
have to decide what
kind of difference you
want to make."

—*Jane Goodall*

```
F  R  A  N  K  L  L  O  Y  D  W  R  I  G  H  T  M  L  C  J
D  R  L  R  J  B  P  R  K  N  S  E  Y  I  Y  G  L  V  T  O
W  D  E  P  S  Y  R  T  A  E  A  E  B  A  I  A  F  E  B  H
I  J  Q  D  E  U  J  I  T  L  L  T  W  N  H  K  N  L  B  N
L  X  C  I  E  R  S  A  G  S  P  G  T  S  X  O  B  E  E  D
L  J  Q  G  L  R  G  A  E  H  N  H  R  U  T  P  Z  A  N  R
I  X  A  J  A  L  I  R  N  I  A  A  N  G  R  Y  C  N  J  O
A  W  T  C  L  L  P  C  M  B  M  M  N  A  E  N  K  O  A  C
M  L  A  I  K  S  B  E  K  D  A  I  Y  N  D  L  E  R  M  K
F  A  B  L  I  I  H  E  O  D  H  N  T  O  A  E  N  R  I  E
A  I  R  V  T  T  E  O  R  S  O  I  T  S  U  O  R  O  N  F
U  C  L  K  S  D  G  R  A  T  H  U  S  H  T  N  E  O  S  E
L  E  W  E  T  R  I  W  O  W  E  A  G  L  O  P  G  S  P  L
K  N  N  T  U  W  T  S  I  B  N  I  A  L  R  N  X  E  O  L
N  R  C  H  B  R  A  L  N  O  I  W  N  K  A  D  Y  V  C  E
E  A  T  B  E  J  E  I  J  E  M  N  T  S  A  S  K  E  K  R
R  T  Q  K  U  L  V  U  N  A  Y  D  S  O  T  E  S  L  D  R
G  E  O  R  G  E  E  A  S  T  M  A  N  O  D  E  B  T  D  O
L  O  U  I  S  A  R  M  S  T  R  O  N  G  N  X  I  O  B  R
B  E  N  J  A  M  I  N  F  R  A  N  K  L  I  N  N  M  S
```

influential americans

ALBERT EINSTEIN
BENJAMIN FRANKLIN
BENJAMIN SPOCK
BILL GATES
BOOKER T. WASHINGTON
BRIGHAM YOUNG
ELEANOR ROOSEVELT
ELI WHITNEY
ELVIS PRESLEY

ERNEST HEMINGWAY
FRANK LLOYD WRIGHT
FREDERICK DOUGLASS
GEORGE EASTMAN
JACKIE ROBINSON
JOHN D. ROCKEFELLER
JONAS SALK

LOUIS ARMSTRONG
MARK TWAIN
NAT TURNER
RALPH NADER
SAM WALTON
SUSAN B. ANTHONY
THURGOOD MARSHALL
WALT DISNEY
WILLIAM FAULKNER

vital virtues

Channel your inner Benjamin Franklin, who in his autobiography listed the essential virtues he believed would mold his character. What virtues are most vital to you? What makes you your best self?

. . . .

. . . .

. . . .

. . . .

. . . .

. . . .

. . . .

. . . .

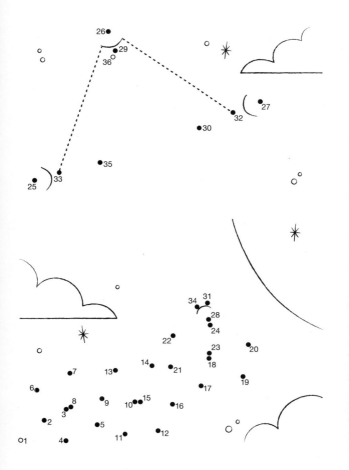

55

find and circle

Seven words starting and ending in "B"	⊘○○○○○○
Three school subjects	○○○
Two sources of poultry	○○
Two North American countries	○○
Eating utensil for soup	○

"We are each gifted in a
unique and important way.
It is our privilege and our
adventure to discover our
own special light."

—*Mary Dunbar*

OFFLINE By Anna Gundlach

ACROSS

1. Spots in front of TVs
6. Cleans the floor
10. "If only ..."
11. Luxury boat
12. Hardly verbose
13. ___ in the right direction
14. Device that the average American adult will spend more than three hours a day with
16. Furious rage
17. Fondue vessel
18. One way to be less distracted by your 14-Across
23. ___ polloi
24. Get into a pickle
25. One way to be less distracted by your 14-Across
30. Super-mega
31. Groundbreaking music player first released in 2001
33. Recovery program
34. Make like a horse
35. Ice cream brand called Dreyer's on the West Coast
36. Lauder found at Sephora

DOWN

1. Park yourself
2. Is in the black
3. Unwavering
4. Lay into
5. Shepherd formerly of "The View"
6. Crush, like food
7. Armed marine creatures
8. Amazing new sports player
9. City near Tampa, familiarly
11. Go on and on and on and on ...
15. Core principle
18. "Yeah, I bet ..."
19. Undermind, like a nefarious plan
20. Disgustingly soiled
21. Weasel or stoat with a white winter coat
22. Recurrent literary devices
26. Progressive and Swing
27. Snag
28. "Get started, now!"
29. It gets honed with a strop
32. Gender-specific pronoun

"Life offers you a thousand chances . . . all you have to do is take one."

—*Frances Mayes*

find and circle

Five dairy products	⊘○○○○
Four joints	○○○○
Three colors starting with "G"	○○○
Two lighter-than-air gases	○○
Two four-letter mammals starting with "M"	○○

"Don't look at your feet to see if
you are doing it right. Just dance."

—*Anne Lamott*

```
S E E F R I E N D S R A Z H Z T K K P S
W A S H T H E C A R L E R R A N D S P Q
A X D L R T R E A D T H E P A P E R H F
T P Z Q N A E Q V L W W F A R A E G A Z
C N S A H K L S X X X Y V R C Y L P P C
H D B B G E A U H W C I W J H B A V P O
M A L M R A X L K P H U J P U I U X Y F
O T E A I N A D F K L V R Q R L N N H F
V E D K L A T H A A Z A W E C L D O O E
I N S E L P I S L R M B Y G H S R W U E
E I H P O Z O L C R M I B G S V Y O R S
S G O L U K N E H H E W L Y R U G R S H
E H P A T M T E O N D X A Y S O N K O O
G T P N S Q B P R Q N D E T D I U D O P
H O I S O S O I E V I K J R P I S N A T
S A N G H E F N S R D Z Y Y C S N W D Y
B I G B R E A K F A S T Y U R I O N C I
M O W T H E L A W N P S G V U T S G E U
Q G N V N B S A T U R D A Y N I P E Z R
D R I N K W I N E G R O C E R Y S H O P
```

weekends

BIG BREAKFAST
CHORES
CHURCH
COFFEE SHOP
DATE NIGHT
DRINK WINE
ERRANDS
EXERCISE
FAMILY DINNER
FRIDAY

GRILL OUT
GROCERY SHOP
HAPPY HOUR
LAUNDRY
MAKE PLANS
MOW THE LAWN
NO WORK
PAY BILLS
PLAYGROUND
READ THE PAPER

RELAXATION
SATURDAY
SEE FRIENDS
SHOPPING
SLEEP IN
SUNDAY
TAKE A NAP
WASH THE CAR
WATCH MOVIES

find and circle

Eight sports	⊘○○○○○○○
Three female relatives (four-letter min.)	○○○
Three four-letter words starting with "J"	○○○
Underground part of a tree	○
Beach material	○

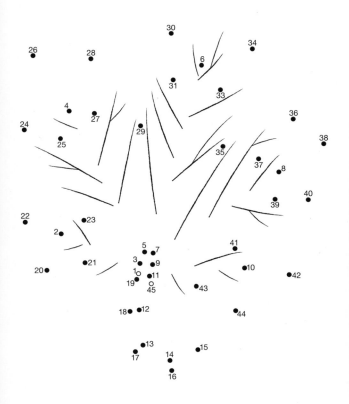

giving back

Think about what causes mean the most to you.
What issues are you passionate about? Write down
some ideas below and then research organizations
that align with your passions to see how you can
support their work. Giving back is one of the best
ways to boost happiness and satisfaction.

. . . .

. . . .

. . . .

. . . .

. . . .

. . . .

. . . .

. . . .

"Learn to enjoy every minute of your life. Be happy now. Don't wait for something outside of yourself to make you happy in the future."

—*Earl Nightingale*

find and circle

Seven mammals starting with "B" ⊘○○○○○○

Five four-letter colors ○○○○○

The weekend ○○

Two five-letter gases ○○

Groom's partner in a wedding ○

"The inward journey
is about finding
your own fullness,
something that
no one else can
take away."

—*Deepak Chopra*

self-care By Anna Gundlach

ACROSS

1. Put some chips in the pot
6. Foil material replaced by aluminum
9. Rapper with the 9x Platinum #1 single "Bodak Yellow"
11. Person from Copenhagen
12. *Mediterranean volcano
13. WWW part
14. Cartoony response to a mouse
15. Harvested
17. *Menacing snakelike fish
19. Brainstorming results
22. Like a sarcastic remark
23. *Metaphorical place for imagination
25. Charismatic allure
26. Part of an old-timey cabin's wall
29. Frilly fabric
30. Period for taking care of oneself ... or a three-word hint for the answers to this puzzle's starred clues
33. Abbr. at the top of a memo
34. Squid or squirrel
35. ___ Moines, Iowa
36. Campus leaders

DOWN

1. Highest point
2. Sports writer and statistician Silver
3. Arduous journey
4. Summer clock setting in NJ
5. Uproarious racket
6. Taiwan's capital
7. "Absolutely!"
8. Piece of debris from a Christmas tree
10. Roseanne of "Roseanne"
11. Wrestler/actor Johnson, a.k.a. The Rock
16. Like a Monday crossword
17. Emmy-winning TV drama set in the 1960s
18. ___ buco (veal dish)
19. "That's so nice to hear!"
20. Widen, like a pupil
21. Makes into law
24. Humorist Bombeck
26. Kind of bean first found in Peru
27. Arabian country
28. Hair products
31. Wrap up
32. Knot up

"Follow what you are genuinely passionate about and let that guide you to your destination."

—*Diane Sawyer*

T J S A T U R D A Y I T
X E S A C C O R D C N N
B C N U G R E E N I D E
E B Z T N G O L D V I S
N G R A Y D F I T I A W
T K V J T L A N K C N E
J A R C T I C Y J K V N
P A C I F I C Z D E N T

find and circle

Five four-letter words that rhyme with "gent"	⊘○○○○
Three oceans	○○○
Three colors starting with "G"	○○○
Three Honda models	○○○
The weekend	○○

breaking barriers

Reflect on the last time you pushed yourself out of your comfort zone. What prompted it? Has it been a long time since you've tested your boundaries?

. . . .

. . . .

. . . .

. . . .

. . . .

. . . .

. . . .

. . . .

. . . .

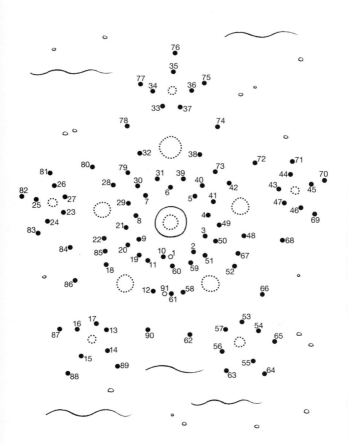

"You must go on adventures to find out where you belong."

—*Sue Fitzmaurice*

prioritizing self-care

Self-discovery can't happen when your physical and emotional reserves are empty. You cannot pour from an empty cup. Reflect on what calms and restores you. Can you make time for one of those things this week?

values By Anna Gundlach

ACROSS

1. *Part of 21-Across representing O
5. Almost-unknown celebrities
10. Elba of "The Wire"
12. A little extra pizzazz
13. Popular payment app owned by PayPal
14. Coffee additive
15. Curvy road section
16. Bread for a Reuben
18. Mined find
19. Had a Reuben, say
20. Schnozzle
21. 7-4-9-3-5 (When solved using the starred clues, a set of values used to live a good, fulfilled life)
24. Verb used in a game of Battleship
25. Simmering setting
26. Will Ferrell Christmas movie
27. Anti-drug ad, say
28. Get some color on the beach
31. Tenor, e.g.
33. Food rated in alarms
35. Scandalous company in 2002 news
36. Like you and me
37. Has to have
38. Hereditary element

DOWN

1. *Part of 21-Across representing L
2. Praising poetry
3. Coffee containers
4. Lip
5. RX portion
6. Singers Bega or Reed
7. "All set over here"
8. Few and far between
9. *Part of 21-Across representing A
11. A li'l bit
17. Hoots and hollers
19. MacGuffin in the first Indiana Jones movie
20. This very moment
21. "Circles" and "Rockstar" singer Post ___
22. Doing unstoppably great
23. Sports leader
24. *Part of 21-Across representing M
27. The English call them biros
28. "Person of the Year" magazine
29. Mathematician Turing
30. *Part of 21-Across representing R
32. Common whitefish
34. Greeting from a loved one

"Define success on your
own terms, achieve
it by your own rules,
and build a life you're
proud to live."

—*Anne Sweeney*

A M U N C L E X O M B V
K U O C A R Z R D I R Z
N A N T Z K E X A C O R
I B O T H H V Z R H T E
E O O J T E J V O I H T
C V N A X Z R A L G E S
E E F B U S J N O A R I
C O U S I N V N C N V S

find and circle

Eight relatives (four-letter min.)	⊘○○○○○○○
Three three-letter motor vehicles	○○○
Two eight-letter U.S. states	○○
Opposite of below	○
Time 12 hours from midnight	○

"Self-care is giving the world
the best of you, instead of
what's left of you."

—*Katie Reed*

```
S  S  E  L  F  E  S  T  E  E  M  L  B  R  U  D  Y  R  P  P
B  O  U  N  D  A  R  I  E  S  V  D  S  C  V  Y  K  F  K  A
T  A  C  I  L  O  G  D  Q  M  R  E  L  I  D  S  L  R  A  S
R  R  U  A  A  H  X  E  V  P  T  F  A  N  E  F  I  B  P  S
C  E  I  V  A  A  W  L  M  R  J  E  V  T  N  U  X  A  O  I
W  E  P  G  Z  F  E  U  B  O  A  N  O  I  I  N  S  N  C  V
T  T  M  R  G  N  X  S  D  J  R  S  I  M  A  C  I  E  O  E
K  B  Y  P  E  E  A  I  E  E  C  E  D  A  L  T  H  U  D  A
J  E  A  F  A  S  R  O  C  C  O  M  A  C  E  I  I  R  E  G
A  U  B  G  I  T  S  N  N  T  U  E  N  Y  I  O  N  O  P  G
K  N  Q  T  G  X  H  I  P  I  C  C  C  M  R  N  N  S  E  R
T  C  R  K  Z  A  E  Y  O  O  H  H  E  O  Q  A  E  I  N  E
T  O  S  Q  I  P  G  G  T  N  D  A  G  G  N  L  R  S  D  S
P  N  J  G  E  I  H  E  F  P  P  N  H  M  I  Q  C  C  E  S
H  S  Q  S  U  B  C  O  N  S  C  I  O  U  S  E  H  R  N  I
O  C  D  C  L  O  S  U  R  E  Q  S  Z  E  G  O  I  R  C  V
B  I  S  T  R  E  S  S  T  H  V  M  B  V  C  K  L  O  E  E
I  O  O  S  E  L  F  A  W  A  R  E  N  E  S  S  D  W  A  U
A  U  P  O  V  H  D  S  H  R  I  N  K  B  U  L  F  L  Z  D
C  S  E  M  J  U  W  C  T  K  D  S  F  O  C  R  W  E  N  P
```

talk therapy

AVOIDANCE

BAGGAGE

BOUNDARIES

CLOSURE

CODEPENDENCE

COUCH

DEFENSE
  MECHANISM

DELUSION

DENIAL

DYSFUNCTIONAL

EGO

EMPATHY

INNER CHILD

INTIMACY

NEUROSIS

PASSIVE-
  AGGRESSIVE

PHOBIA

PROJECTION

REPRESSION

SELF-AWARENESS

SELF-ESTEEM

SHRINK

STRESS

SUBCONSCIOUS

TRIGGER

UNCONSCIOUS

"Never limit yourself because of others' limited imagination; never limit others because of your own limited imagination."

—*Mae Jemison*

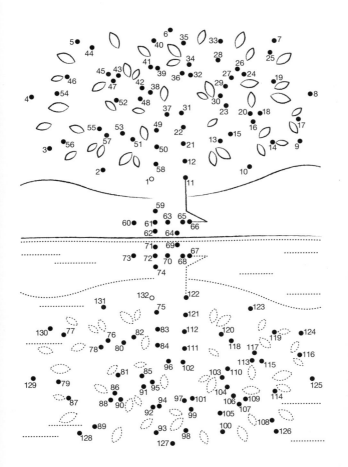

self-compassion

We all want to be compassionate people, but while we often find ways to be caring toward others, we don't reserve the same kindness for ourselves. Think about a time recently when you were compassionate toward a friend. Now think about how you could support yourself the same way.

. . . .

. . . .

. . . .

. . . .

. . . .

. . . .

. . . .

. . . .

"If everyone else
around you is worthy
of care and attention,
then so are you."

—*Dee Waldeck*

zen By Anna Gundlach

ACROSS

1. "That's more than I needed to know!"
4. Sends a dupe email to
7. Speechless state
10. Took home the gold
11. Pieces in the Smithsonian
12. 747, e.g.
13. 401(k) alternative
14. With 8-Down, "My Little Chickadee" costar
15. Braying beast
16. *Summery outdoors social gathering
19. Speak like you're drunk
20. Except
21. *Grand Canyon and Niagara Falls
25. Christmas tree
26. Star Wars sister
28. *Instruction given by an expert of a particular discipline
32. 2016 Olympics host
33. Run out of juice
34. Series with "NY"and "Cyber" spinoffs
35. Hoopla
36. Kyoto currency
37. Gunpowder green, e.g.

38. Path to enlightenment, and what can come before the first words in the answers to the starred clues
39. "To the utmost" suffix
40. Govt. ID

DOWN

1. Pieces of a nest
2. Aesop's conclusions
3. Stuck with a boring routine
4. Made an appearance
5. Fruit for Thanksgiving
6. Rise to the challenge
7. Just a little open
8. See 14-Across
9. Online DIY craft market
17. Early version
18. Even once
22. Hippie's coloring method
23. Respond to
24. Part of XOXO
27. From Loas or Kyrgyzstan
28. "I'm Yours" since Jason
29. Congressional helper
30. Any moment now
31. Small change

109

"Tell me, what is it you plan
to do with your one wild and
precious life?"

—*Mary Oliver*

notes

notes

solutions

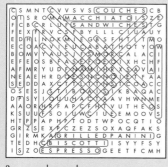

3   word search

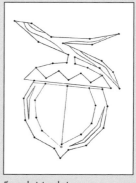

5   dot to dot

10   spot the differences

12   crossword

114

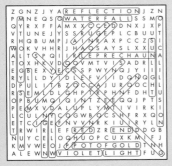

15 word search

BASKETBALL,
WRESTLING, FOOTBALL,
RUGBY, POLO—HEALTH,
HUTCH, HUNCH,
HIGH, HUSH—POUND,
HOUND, SOUND—
HOOVER—CRUST

16 word roundup

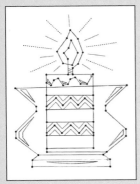

19 dot to dot

24 spot the differences

SOLUTIONS

B	O	P	S			I	M	B	I	B	E
O	N	L	Y			N	U	R	S	E	S
S	T	A	N			S	T	A	T	I	C
C	O	N	C	E	P	T	I	O	N		
	P	E	S	C	I		N	O	G		
			O	R	E						
	S	A	T		A	L	A	M	O		
	C	R	E	A	T	I	V	I	T	Y	
S	O	M	A	L	I		A	L	T	O	
P	R	E	S	T	O		S	E	E	D	
A	N	D	E	A	N		T	Y	R	A	

26   crossword

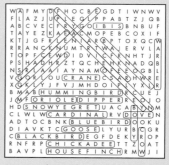

29   word search

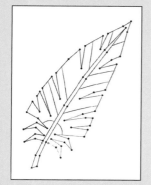

31   dot to dot

36   spot the differences

116

38 crossword

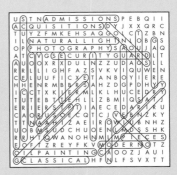

41 word search

BLUE, PINK, GOLD,
GRAY, TEAL—
PORTUGAL, PAKISTAN,
PANAMA, POLAND,
PERU—TOWNSHEND,
DALTREY—CANOE,
OCEAN—YEAR, WEEK

42 word roundup

44 dot to dot

48 spot the differences

50 crossword

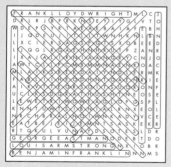

53 word search

55 dot to dot

118

BATHTUB, BLURB,
BARB, BULB, BLOB,
BLAB, BIB—SCIENCE,
HISTORY, MATH—
CHICKEN, TURKEY—
MEXICO, CANADA—
SPOON

57   word roundup

60   spot the differences

S	O	F	A	S			M	O	P	S
I	W	I	S	H		Y	A	C	H	T
T	E	R	S	E		A	S	T	E	P
	S	M	A	R	T	P	H	O	N	E
		I	R	E			P	O	T	
O	F	F	L	I	N	E	T	I	M	E
H	O	I			E	R	R			
S	I	L	E	N	T	M	O	D	E	
U	L	T	R	A		I	P	O	D	S
R	E	H	A	B		N	E	I	G	H
E	D	Y	S			E	S	T	E	E

62   crossword

CHEESE, BUTTER,
YOGURT, CREAM,
MILK—ELBOW, ANKLE,
WRIST, KNEE—GREEN,
GOLD, GRAY—
HYDROGEN,
HELIUM—MOLE, MULE

65   word roundup

119

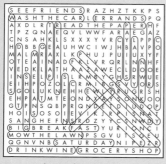

67 word search

SOFTBALL, FOOTBALL,
CRICKET, TENNIS,
HOCKEY, BOXING,
RUGBY, POLO—
MOTHER, NIECE,
AUNT—JAVA, JAZZ,
JOKE—ROOT—SAND

68 word roundup

69 dot to dot

BUFFALO, BABOON,
BEAVER, BADGER,
BOBCAT, BEAR, BAT—
BLUE, GOLD, PINK,
TEAL, GRAY—SATURDAY,
SUNDAY—ARGON,
RADON—BRIDE

74 word roundup

76 spot the differences

78 crossword

TENT, BENT, DENT, SENT, WENT—

PACIFIC, INDIAN, ARCTIC—GREEN, GOLD, GRAY—

ACCORD, CIVIC, FIT—

SATURDAY, SUNDAY

81 word roundup

83 dot to dot

88 spot the differences

90 crossword

BROTHER, MOTHER,
FATHER, SISTER,
COUSIN, UNCLE,
NIECE, AUNT—VAN,
BUS, CAR—MICHIGAN,
COLORADO—ABOVE—
NOON

93 word roundup

95 word search

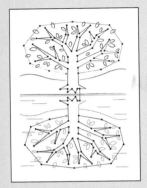

97 dot to dot

102 spot the differences

104 crossword

108 spot the differences

Andrews McMeel Publishing
a division of Andrews McMeel Universal
1130 Walnut Street, Kansas City, Missouri 64106

www.andrewsmcmeel.com

20 21 22 23 24 RLP 10 9 8 7 6 5 4 3 2 1

ISBN: 978-1-5248-6055-4

Editor: Allison Adler
Art Director: Julie Barnes
Production Editor: Dave Shaw
Production Manager: Tamara Haus

ATTENTION: SCHOOLS AND BUSINESSES
Andrews McMeel books are available at quantity
discounts with bulk purchase for educational,
business, or sales promotional use. For information,
please e-mail the Andrews McMeel Publishing
Special Sales Department: specialsales@amuniversal.com.